FAQ
TEEN LIFE™

FREQUENTLY ASKED QUESTIONS ABOUT

Date Rape

Tamra
Orr

ROSEN
PUBLISHING®
New York

Published in 2007 by The Rosen Publishing Group, Inc.
29 East 21st Street, New York, NY 10010

Copyright © 2007 by The Rosen Publishing Group, Inc.

First Edition

Library of Congress Cataloging-in-Publication Data

Orr, Tamra.
Frequently asked questions about date rape / Tamra Orr. — 1st ed.
p. cm. — (FAQ : teen life)
ISBN-13: 978-1-4042-1972-4
ISBN-10: 1-4042-1972-2
1. Date rape—United States.
2. Date rape—United States—Prevention. I. Title.
HV6561.O77 2007
364.15'32—dc22

2006033648

Manufactured in the United States of America

Contents

Introduction

Many people have the mistaken idea that a person can be raped only by a stranger, but that isn't true. Date rape occurs when two people get together socially and one person forces the other to have sex. No matter what kind of relationship the two people have, no one has the right to force another to have sex against his or her will. It doesn't matter if the two people are dating, have had consensual (mutually agreed upon) sex before, or are even married. Just because a person agrees to go on a date with another person, it doesn't mean that he or she wants to have sex with that person that very night or ever. Just because you are married to or regularly sleeping with someone doesn't mean you have to have sex if you don't want to at any particular time.

Date rape is not a new problem. It may be hard to believe that women and girls can be raped by their dates, since most of us think of rape as something a man does to a person he does not know. In movies or on TV, we see rapists stalking their victims through dark alleys. Unfortunately, date rape is not a rare occurrence. According to the National Victim Center, one out of every six adult women has experienced either complete or attempted rape in her lifetime. Seven out of ten rape survivors know their rapists, according to the National Center for Injury Prevention and Control. According to the 2004 National Crime Victimization

The popular image of a rapist is a shady character who attacks an unknown victim. In fact, most rape cases involve people who know each other.

Following a sexual assault or rape, most survivors experience intense emotions that are difficult to face.

Survey, 67 percent of rape victims are attacked by people they know, such as a friend, a date, or even a husband, while almost 80 percent of all reported rapes are acquaintance rapes, or rapes that happen between people who already know each other (including dates).

Rape victims experience many different emotions after an attack. They feel shame, confusion, fear, and even guilt. They may wonder if they somehow caused the rape. But it's extremely important to know that rape is never the victim's fault. No one has the right to force you to have sex if you don't want to. Rape is a violent crime, and rapists are criminals. The rapist is the one who has done something wrong, not the victim.

Being raped is a traumatic experience. One basic human right is that a person has control over his or her body. When that right is violated, the person feels as if he or she has no control over anything. Physical injuries heal, but emotional scars can last for a long time. When a person is raped on a date, it can be more difficult because the rapist is someone the victim knows and trusted enough to go out on a date with. After the attack, the victim may have to see the assailant at school every day. Rape victims also must decide whether or not to report the attack. This is a personal choice, and there is no right or wrong decision. It is an especially hard decision for victims of date rape. The survivors may fear other people's reactions. They may feel that others are less likely to believe them—especially if the attacker is someone popular and thought of as a nice person.

A note about the terminology used in this book. A victim is anyone who is raped, but that person is also called a survivor. This book refers to people who have been raped as both victims and survivors. This entry usually refers to survivors as "she" and assailants as "he," but both women and men can be raped. And though most assailants are men, women can also commit rape.

WHY DOES DATE RAPE OCCUR?

Nobody is truly certain why rape happens. Some say our society—including the often violent and sexist images and messages provided every day by mass media like films, television, popular music, advertising, and video games—teaches men to rape. Others believe just the opposite—that men are naturally violent and that societal restrictions and norms of behavior are what keep most men from committing rape.

It is important to avoid the temptation of pointing a finger at any one factor, such as the media or pornography, as the cause for something as complicated as rape. But looking at how our society views men and women can give us an idea of what rape is really about.

Guns and Dolls

If you are a girl, you may have been given baby dolls to play with when you were little. If you are a boy, you

Some say social stereotypes encourage girls and women to be viewed as playthings instead of people.

probably grew up playing with footballs, G.I. Joes, and toy guns. Have you ever wondered why? To some extent, these toys represent and reinforce stereotypes of boys and girls, their typical behavior, and what they're supposed to be interested in. Stereotypes are commonly held beliefs that may or may not be true. They often lead us to assume things about girls and boys that are not true.

Stereotypes about boys usually focus on aggression and action. For example, many people believe that all boys like sports. Many boys do like sports, but there are also many who do not. And there are lots of girls who like and excel at sports. Many people believe that all boys like to fight or that boys should solve their problems by using violence. This also is not true.

Stereotypes about girls often show them as passive and weak, not strong and assertive. Girls are expected to be nurturing and emotional, but these are qualities that males can have as well. Seeing women as weak and helpless is one way of stereotyping them as victims.

These stereotypes influence the way young men and women perceive themselves and one another. This can lead to problems when they begin dating. Boys may believe that they are supposed to want sex all the time. They may also believe that girls are weak, indecisive, and easily influenced or controlled. This coupled with a perceived lack of interest in sex makes many guys think that even if a woman clearly says she doesn't want to have sex, she can be persuaded, bullied, or forced into it anyway. These false beliefs can sometimes lead to date rape.

In some sports, guys are rewarded for being violent and physically aggressive. But football is not the same as life.

Girls often share these beliefs. For example, if a boy is being too aggressive, the girl may not tell him to stop even if she is uncomfortable because she has been taught that it is okay for boys to be aggressive. And if he becomes violent and tries to rape her, she may not know how to fight back because, over the years, she has been taught that girls are not supposed to fight and that the will and desires of a man always take precedence over those of a woman.

We all know that women have come a long way toward equality. There are more and more women doing the jobs that used to be done only by men. But that doesn't mean that all the negative stereotypes about men and women are gone. Women do compete with men in the workplace. But many women think they are still supposed to be more passive when it comes to dating. Think about it: When it comes to making plans for a date, who still makes the first phone call? Most of the time, in a heterosexual relationship, it's the guy. And even though women can now wear suits to work, they are still supposed to look somewhat sexy. But not too sexy. Many people will blame a woman for any unwanted sexual attention she receives or even sexual assaults if she is dressed in a certain way. They will think that, somehow, a woman was asking for trouble.

Date rape happens because many guys believe these gender stereotypes. They believe they should fight to get what they want (in this case, sex). They believe that real men have a lot of sex when they are young. They believe that women are passive, so they must be forced into having sex.

Dressing in a sexy outfit is a way to get attention, but no outfit is a green light to touch another person or initiate sex without her consent.

Myths and Facts

About Date Rape

 A woman can only be raped by a stranger with a weapon who lurks in dark alleys.
Fact ➡ This idea is false. According to the 2004 National Crime Victimization Survey, 67 percent of rape survivors are attacked by people they know such as a friend, a date, or even a husband.

 A woman is only playing hard to get when she says no. Fact ➡ When a woman says no, she means no. Guys need to respect a woman's decision.

Men rape only when they don't get enough sex.
Fact ➡ When a man rapes, he does not want sex. Rape is a violent crime committed by a person who craves power and control over someone else.

 Date rape doesn't exist. Girls claim rape only because they feel guilty or regretful about having sex.

Fact ➡️ Anytime someone forces another to have sex against her will, it is rape. It doesn't matter if they are on a first date, have dated for months, or are married. Very few women lie about being raped.

Once a girl has agreed to have sex with a guy, she can never say no to him again.
Fact ➡️ A woman has the right to say no at any time, no matter what their previous sexual relationship or romantic history.

It's always the woman's fault if she is raped.
Fact ➡️ Rape is a crime and is never the victim's fault. Like all crimes, the criminal is at fault.

A woman who flirts with a man signals that she wants to have sex with him. Fact ➡️ When two people go out on a date, they want to have a good time and enjoy each other's company. Flirting is a fun part of dating, but a woman who flirts with a man is not indicating that she wants to have sex.

If a man spends a lot of money on a date, he is entitled to have sex with her. Fact ➡️ Nothing a man does, including spending money on a date, entitles him to sex. Sex takes places between two consenting adults. If a woman is forced to have sex against her will, it is rape.

Boys are rarely raped. Fact ➡ Anyone can be a victim of rape—men, women, children, homosexuals, and heterosexuals. According to the 2004 National Crime Victimization Survey, about one out of every ten victims of sexual assault is male. It is estimated that 18 percent of rape victims are under age twelve and 44 percent are under age eighteen.

A woman who dates a lot of men, wears sexy clothing, and stays out late has no one to blame but herself if she is raped. Fact ➡ No matter how a person acts or dresses, it doesn't mean she has resigned control over her body. Nobody has the right to force her to do something she doesn't want to. Plus, what you think someone's outfit is saying may not be at all what the wearer thinks it's saying (if she thinks it's saying anything in the first place).

A woman who goes somewhere alone with a man must be willing to have sex with him. Fact ➡ In a romantic relationship, it's perfectly natural and acceptable to want to spend intimate time alone together. However, a woman who wants to be alone with a man does not necessarily want to have sex with him. If she says she doesn't, then she doesn't.

A person can never return to a normal life after being raped. Fact ➡ Although being raped is a highly traumatic experience, a person can recover from it and live a happy and fulfilling life.

When guys listen to these stereotypes instead of to their dates, they are in danger of committing date rape. When a guy expects to have sex on a date, he is forgetting that there's another person involved, who may or may not have different expectations, but whose opinion and wishes must always be sought and respected. That other person has an absolute right to choose whether or not to have sex. A guy who believes the stereotypes will ignore his date's signals. He will stop listening to what she's saying. He will assume he knows what's best for her, though in reality he is only thinking of his own wants and needs.

The Role of the Media

The media (movies, television, magazines, and advertisements) play an important role in how society views women. The media often show women in stereotypical roles. They are shown as weak and submissive or as objects or property owned by men. Think of the last movie you watched, or the last magazine you flipped though, or the last commercial you saw. How are women shown? Do they often wear very revealing clothing or always seem to need men to rescue them from a dangerous enemy or their own mistakes? What kind of role do they play other than to stand there and look beautiful? These images often send a message to society that women are weak and do not have minds of their own.

Women are seen as helpless. In most action movies and TV shows, the men are the ones out chasing the bad guys and saving the world. Where are the women? Often, they are victims. And it's up to the men to help them or save them. Sometimes the women are the beautiful girlfriends of the men, standing around and looking pretty. They are often thought of as possessions that the men have, like a sports car or a gun. They can be traded among men or discarded for newer models, just like any consumer goods. In movies and television, the women often don't do anything but support the men. The women are seen as entirely passive.

Women are portrayed as sexual objects. Pornographic magazines and movies are full of pictures of naked women. They are there to give men sexual pleasure. That's all. They are not shown as real people. They do not have opinions and they don't talk—or if they do speak, it is only to utter empty-headed statements that reflect the fantasies of male writers and viewers. They are simply sexual objects. Many men consider these women to be the ideal. They have been taught that the best woman is one with no voice or personality. But women are people, not objects. And women (like all people) deserve respect.

In today's media, women are often seen but not heard. We get the message that the thoughts and opinions of women are unimportant.

Women's bodies are like products. Advertising uses pictures of beautiful women to sell products. For example, many companies show women's legs to sell cigarettes. Advertising like this promotes two false ideas: 1) That buying a certain product will get you a beautiful woman, and 2) That you can get a beautiful woman as easily as you can buy a pack of cigarettes. Neither of these things is true. It doesn't matter how much money you spend on a date. It doesn't matter how much you want a woman's body. It's her body, and she has the right to decide what she does with it, with whom, where, and when.

Many people are bombarded with images from the media in their everyday lives. Almost every American home has at least one television set. More and more people are going to the movies. We can't go outside without seeing an ad on a billboard, bus shelter, or promotional postcard. Some boys and girls may have a hard time telling the difference between the images presented in the media and real life. But it's important to realize that the images seen in the media are not real. They often do not show real-life situations. Often these images are used to sell a product. Look around at the people you know. Do they look, act, or talk like the people seen in movies, television, or ads?

Despite what the media show, women are not objects to be bought and owned. Rape occurs when men stop seeing women as people and instead see them as objects.

TWO

HOW CAN YOU DEFEND YOURSELF AGAINST DATE RAPE?

Recent generations of women have taken great strides toward gender equality. As women have learned to compete in a man's world—taking care of themselves, building careers, and living independently—they have also had to learn to defend themselves in a way that once only men did. In recent years, more women have begun to work out, take self-defense classes, and carry defensive weapons like pepper spray, whistles, or piercing alarms. It's sad that this kind of preparedness and vigilance are necessary simply to be out and about in our world, but this is the reality and it must be taken into consideration.

How to Protect Yourself

Rape is a violent crime; it is a criminal act. Like other crimes of violence, there's the potential that it can happen

Empower yourself by taking a self-defense class. Knowing that you can physically repel an attacker will improve your confidence.

to any of us, more or less at random. Anyone can be a victim of rape, including date rape. Unfortunately, there is no way to make yourself completely safe from sexual assault. But using common sense can make you a lot safer. Here are some suggestions to help reduce your chances of being raped by an acquaintance or a date:

- When going out on a date with someone new, always let your parents or someone responsible know where you will be.
- Take note of the person's body language. Is the person too possessive or controlling? Does he respect your opinions?
- Trust your instincts. If you feel that you are somewhere that is too deserted, suggest going to a place where there are more people. If something feels wrong, just walk away and get to a safe, crowded, public place.
- If you feel a guy is putting pressure on you, tell him that you want him to stop. If he does not listen, try to leave or call for help. Even if you're unsure, anytime you feel uncomfortable, it's better to be safe than sorry.
- Avoid alcohol and drugs. Fifty-five percent of college-age women who reported sexual assaults said they had been drinking or using drugs.
- Make sure you have money with you when you leave the house.
- When you're going to a party where you don't know very many people, invite a few friends to accompany you.
- Avoid being alone with a guy you don't know or trust completely. Surround yourself with a group of trusted

If you are impaired by alcohol, it is more difficult for you to send a clear message of what you do and don't want.

friends when first going out with a new acquaintance. Chances are a guy will not try to commit rape with other people around.

→ Try to establish how far you will go sexually before the date. Ask the guy what he expects from the date. If the guy is expecting something you're not going to do, don't go out with him.

➤ If a guy starts pushing you to go farther than you wish to sexually, use a firm and loud voice to say "No!" Scream and yell if you have to, even if no one seems to be around. It may be enough to deter him and may attract the attention of unseen people nearby.

Be Assertive

Often, girls are more inclined than guys to want to please people and be liked. Some guys will take advantage of that and try to pressure young women into having sex. But girls who know what they want and assert themselves are more likely to be respected. Do not let a guy force you to have sex with him just because he wants you to or tries to pressure you. A guy who pressures you about sex is thinking only of himself. You should be thinking of yourself. Any guy who does not respect your choices doesn't respect you, and he doesn't deserve you.

Learning how to take control of a situation and insist that your wishes be respected will make you more confident in all areas of your life. The more you assert yourself, the better you will feel—and the safer you will be.

Drugs and Alcohol

It is important to be careful about the consumption of alcohol or any other drug, especially if you are with people you do not

With this product, a young woman can test whether her drink has been "spiked," or mixed with a date rape drug.

know. Drugs decrease our ability to judge if a situation is safe or not. If you are drunk or high, you might not realize that your date is coming on too strong or that you have wandered far away from the party.

This does not mean that a woman who was drinking when she was assaulted caused her own rape. Her drinking did not make someone else abuse her. But if you are not drinking, you are more alert and more in control. Being clearheaded can help you avoid, stop, fight off, or escape from an assault.

Just as important, do not stay with a guy who is drunk. If your date seems out of control, look for another way to get home. Just because you began the evening with a guy does not mean you have to stay with him—especially if he makes you feel uncomfortable or puts you in danger.

There is a drug called Rohypnol, or "roofie," that is the most commonly used "date rape drug." The drug is illegal in the United States. It is a powerful sedative that can last up to twelve hours and is slipped into drinks. Since it has no color, taste, or smell, you can swallow it and not know it. According to the Partnership for a Drug-Free America, Rohypnol creates a sleepy, relaxed, and drunk feeling. It can leave a person vulnerable to an assailant. Therefore, be aware of your surroundings. Whenever you are out with other people, you should always pour your own drink and keep a careful watch over it. Not all guys are rapists. It is important to trust people, but trust has to be earned. Until it is, you should be careful.

Many victims have woken up in their own beds or in strange places with a foggy, suspicious feeling after having only one or two drinks. If you suspect that you might have been slipped a roofie, go to your nearest emergency room. The drug will still be in your system for twenty-four hours, and the hospital can do a rape exam to make sure you are okay. They can also collect vital evidence in case you decide you want to press charges, so do not shower and be sure to bring the clothes you were wearing the night before.

Danger Signs in a Date

Studies have shown that a rapist's behavior often follows certain patterns. Although not all rapists exhibit these traits and tendencies, it is wise to watch out for these behaviors and avoid people who engage in them. Some tendencies to be wary of:

- Invasion of your personal space
- A total lack of respect for your feelings
- Constantly telling you that you are wrong
- Always claiming that he knows better than you
- Hostile, controlling, and obsessive behavior
- Desensitization to and acceptance and enjoyment of violence

If you find yourself in a situation that feels dangerous, try to draw attention to yourself. Do not go anywhere alone with someone you do not know or with whom you do not feel comfortable. If you are threatened or attacked, yell, scream, or bang on a wall—whatever it takes to be heard. Make enough noise so that someone will hear you. It is better to make a scene and be

When a guy forces himself on you, it is a warning sign that he does not respect your personal space.

embarrassed than to be assaulted. When interviewed in prison, convicted rapists report that a lot of commotion or activity will deter them from going through with the attack. If they think you're going to put up a fight or make a scene, then they may hold off.

Self-Defense

Self-defense classes are a very healthy, proactive course of training. They increase your strength and your self-confidence—and they are fun. One of the best things about self-defense is that size and strength do not matter. Women and men of all ages and abilities can learn how to defend themselves. Many rape survivors find that learning self-defense helps them rebuild their self-confidence and release some of their tension, fear, and anger. People who know self-defense techniques are better equipped to handle a dangerous situation.

Some people believe that during a sexual assault, it is more dangerous to fight back. No one knows whether or not this is true. But many rapists threaten to kill their victims. Many survivors say that they believed it was a real possibility that their assailant would kill them if they struggled. Trust yourself and your instincts. If you are assaulted, do whatever you have to do to get through the situation. If you can get away, go! If you think you know what you are doing, try to defend yourself. But if your assailant has a weapon, or if he is much bigger and stronger than you are, there may be no way to fight back. Just concentrate on staying alive first and foremost. Rape crisis counselors say this: "If you survived, you did the right thing."

Unfortunately, there is no magic solution that will guarantee your safety. Even the most careful person can become a victim of sexual assault. It does not mean the victim was careless or just let it happen. It just means that the danger is very real, and he or she was unlucky.

chapter three

HOW CAN YOU PREVENT DATE RAPE?

One of the strangest things about date rape is that sometimes men commit date rape without realizing that they have done so. A burglar knows that he or she has stolen something. A car thief knows that he or she is taking someone else's car. A rapist lurking in the bushes or a darkened hallway knows that he intends to rape someone.

When it comes to date rape, however, things aren't that clear cut. A lot of guys honestly believe media messages about women and sex. They think that women really do mean "yes" when they say "no," that they're just being coy or presenting a polite and proper show of modesty and reluctance in order to seem like a good girl. They think that a woman must want sex if she goes somewhere alone with a guy. They think that if a girl flirts with a guy, she must want sex. They think that a girl owes a guy sex if he's spent

Hobart College runs workshops to help male students communicate better with young women. This helps avoid the confusion that can lead to date rape.

money on her. So, when a guy like this forces his date to have sex, he may not even know he's raping her! He thinks he's just doing what guys are supposed to do on dates.

Dating Tips for Guys

Here are some tips for guys to help them avoid any sense of confusion on a date, which could lead to an inadvertent sexual assault. First of all, you should always listen to your date. When a girl says "no," you should believe her and stop—no matter

This man is wearing a T-shirt designed by survivors of sexual abuse. It sends a powerful message that rejects old stereotypes.

how excited you are or how doubtful of the sincerity of her statement. It also doesn't matter how sexy or flirtatious someone acts. If she says "no," accept that and don't take it as an invitation to continue to press until you get a "yes." One "no" is all the answer you need, and you should end the discussion there and move on.

You should avoid drinking alcohol. When you're drunk, you can't think very clearly. You might not notice the hints your date is sending you. You might let yourself get carried away. If you stay sober, you can avoid tragic mistakes like date rape.

You should never expect to have sex on a date, no matter how many times you have been on a date with the person before. Date rape often happens because the guy expects to have sex long before the date even happens. Maybe he's been thinking about it for days. Maybe he's planned the whole evening so it will end with sex. You can't make plans for two people all by yourself. Don't expect sex from your date or think that it's your due, something that's owed you in return for paying for everything. Try to enjoy whatever both of you agree to do on the date and leave it at that. Remember, the point of dating is to have fun and to begin finding out if you and your date really like each other. The point of a date is not sex, and it is certainly not rape.

It is important to remember that, although it is normal to have sexual drives, desires, and needs, our dates are people, too, with their own unique qualities, likes, dislikes, desires, and needs. We all deserve respect when we make decisions about our bodies.

Guys Can Be Victims, Too

Sometimes guys can be forced to have sex against their will, too. It is not the image you see on television and in the media, but it is a real possibility. A man with a gentle disposition, for example, or one who isn't very macho can be intimidated by a woman who comes on strong and bullies him into having sex by insulting his manhood or accusing him of being homosexual if he doesn't agree to it. It can be extremely difficult to resist a girl who is

10 FACTS ABOUT DATE RAPE

1 Date rape occurs when two people get together socially and one person forces the other to have sex. No matter what kind of relationship the two people have, no one has the right to force another to have sex against his or her will. It doesn't matter if the two people are dating, have had consensual (mutually agreed upon) sex before, or are even married.

2 Date rape is not an unfortunate misunderstanding or the result of mixed signals. Rape is a violent crime; it is a criminal act.

3 According to the National Victim Center, one out of every six adult women have experienced either complete or attempted rape in their lifetimes.

4 According to the 2004 National Crime Victimization Survey, 67 percent of rape victims are attacked by people they know, such as a friend, a date, or even a husband.

5 A drug called Rohypnol, or "roofie," is the most commonly used date rape drug. The drug is illegal in the United States. It is a powerful sedative that can last up to twelve hours and is slipped into drinks. Since it has no color, taste, or smell, you can swallow it and not know it. According to the Partnership for a Drug-Free America, Rohypnol creates a sleepy, relaxed, and drunk feeling. It can leave a person vulnerable to an assailant.

6 According to the 2004 National Crime Victimization Survey, about one out of every ten victims of sexual assault is male.

7 Eighteen percent of rape victims are under age twelve, and 44 percent are under age eighteen.

8 Ninety-three percent of women and 86 percent of men who were raped and/or physically assaulted since the age of eighteen were assaulted by a male, according to the 1998 National Violence Against Women Survey.

9 Fifty-five percent of college-age women who reported sexual assaults said they had been drinking or using drugs. This does not mean that a woman who was drinking when she was assaulted caused her own rape. Her drinking did not make someone else abuse her. But if you are not drinking, you are more alert and more in control. Being clearheaded can help you avoid, stop, fight off, or escape from an assault.

10 When interviewed in prison, convicted rapists report that a lot of commotion or activity will deter them from going through with the attack. If they think you're going to put up a fight or make a scene, then they may hold off.

offering herself to you, but often there may be a little voice inside your head telling you that this is a mistake and not what you really want to do. A part of you knows you'll regret it, even if you are physically aroused and attracted to the person. A guy can feel many of the same emotions as girls in this situation: confused, humiliated, frightened, uncertain, and angry.

A girl usually cannot force a guy physically to have sex. But if she talks or shames him into having sex against his will, she commits rape.

Women are not usually the aggressors in rape, but sometimes it does happen. Men can be raped by women and by other men, too (whether they are gay or straight). Date rape can happen between gay men. If you are a man and know you have been raped by a woman or another man, you shouldn't feel ashamed or too embarrassed to get medical, psychological, and legal help. According to the Rape, Abuse, and Incest Network, adult males are the least likely rape victims to report a sexual assault and seek help. This shame, secrecy, and bottling up of emotions will slow your recovery and can lead to depression, extreme anger, sexual problems, and violence. Talk to a counselor or a friend you trust. You were the victim of a violent crime. What has happened to you is not your fault. And it does not make you any less of a man.

WHAT IF IT HAPPENS TO YOU?

If you are a victim of date rape, you will probably feel very confused and upset. A lot of different thoughts will be running through your head. Here are some of the things you might find yourself wondering:

How Could This Happen to Me?

Sometimes we don't want to believe that something so horrible could happen to us. We try to find a reason for it. Rape victims often blame themselves. They think they must have done something wrong. That isn't true. It's not your fault if you were raped. It is the rapist's fault. You can (and should) be angry with him or her. Don't be angry with yourself.

How Could He Have Done This to Me?

We date people we think we like. We date people we think are nice. That makes it hard to believe that something as

Being charming is part of the game for many sexual predators. This may make it even harder to trust people again after you are assaulted.

horrible as date rape really happened. But even guys you think are nice can be rapists. There was no way for you to know what was going to happen. It's not your fault that your date ignored your wishes. He's the one at fault.

How Can I Ever Trust Anyone Else Again?

You trusted your date. He raped you. It's hard to feel good about people after an experience like that. But just because one person is bad doesn't mean that everyone is bad. Maybe there were some subtle danger signals you didn't pick up on. Now you'll have a much sharper eye and a keener sense of what to watch out for. Remember, most people are decent. There are still a lot of people you can trust.

How Can I Ever Trust Myself Again?

You might feel that you made a terrible mistake. You trusted someone you shouldn't have. You liked someone who was mean to you. This may make you feel that you can't do anything right. You might start to feel that any decision you make will be wrong. But it wasn't your fault that someone you liked did something bad. And it doesn't mean that you're imperceptive, gullible, or foolish. You were a victim. A crime is never the victim's fault.

Healing the Wounds

Rape is an extremely traumatic experience. Rape damages the body and the emotions. While physical injuries will heal, emotional wounds take a longer time to heal, but it will happen. Here are some things you can do to help with the healing process:

- One of the best things to do is to talk to someone about your feelings. You can speak with a professional counselor or someone close to you, such as a friend, a sibling, or your parents.
- It may be very difficult to open up to someone about what happened. You may feel ashamed, confused, and angered by what happened, but keeping these emotions bottled up will only make it harder to heal.
- You can also call a rape crisis center. The person who answers the phone is a trained expert in handling rape trauma. He or she will always believe you. Rape crisis counselors know all about date rape.

Rape Crisis Centers

You can get the phone number of a rape crisis center by looking in the phone book under Rape. Be sure to check both the white pages and the yellow pages. Or you can call the operator and ask for the number of a rape crisis center.

A sexual assault is an emotionally overwhelming experience. It is important that the victim not suffer alone.

When you call the center, you can talk about anything you want. The counselor you talk to will never tell anyone what you said unless you want him or her to. He or she will stay on the phone with you as long as you want and help you figure out exactly what happened to you. She or he can give you advice about finding other people to talk to—a therapist, a minister or rabbi, a sympathetic friend, a parent.

Getting Medical Attention

After a sexual assault, it is very important to see a doctor. Pregnancy, sexually transmitted diseases (STDs), and injuries are all easier to deal with if they are discovered early. Many conditions are easy to treat in an early stage but can cause major problems if left untreated. It may frighten you to consider this possibility, but it must be addressed. If you have confided in a friend or family member, ask him or her to go to the doctor with you. Having someone there with you will make it easier.

Even if you choose not to tell anyone about the assault, you still need to take care of yourself. Maybe you know a doctor or a clinic that you or a friend has visited. If there is a Planned Parenthood in your town, call for an appointment. Planned Parenthood treats men, too. Many hospitals have walk-in clinics. If you are not sure where to go, look in the yellow pages under Women's Health Care, Medical Care, or Victims' Services.

If you are the victim of a sexual assault, it's important that you see a doctor to treat any physical injuries you may have sustained.

If you go to a doctor immediately after the assault, do not bathe or wash before you go. The doctor or nurse will take samples of bodily fluids and hair, which can be used as evidence if you decide to report the crime to the police. (You do not have to make that decision while you are in the hospital.) If a certain amount of time has passed since the assault, the hospital will not be able to collect evidence.

The confidentiality of medical care varies from state to state. If you are concerned that your parents or a child protection agency will be informed about your assault or abuse, call the Rape, Abuse, and Incest National Network (RAINN) hotline at (800) 656-HOPE (4673) or Childhelp USA at (800) 4-A-CHILD (422-4453) to find out about the laws in your state.

When you arrive at the hospital or medical center, tell the person at the desk that you were sexually assaulted. You will be taken to a private area and seen immediately by a nurse or doctor. He or she will ask you questions about the attack. You may be embarrassed to answer them, but it is important to be honest so that you can be treated properly. The doctor is there to help you, not to judge you.

First you will be treated for any injury that requires immediate attention. You will then be brought to a private examining room. If you are a woman, it is necessary to have a pelvic exam, similar to the one given at a gynecologist's office. This is usually done by a female doctor or nurse who has been specially trained to deal with assault/rape survivors. A counselor, social worker, or volunteer may also be there to offer comfort and support.

To a person who has just been sexually assaulted, a pelvic exam can feel like even more intrusion and humiliation. Though it will not be a pleasant experience, the doctor will try to be as gentle and respectful as possible. She will explain each step of the procedure before it happens.

The doctor or nurse will write notes about your condition. She will give you two injections of antibiotics to help protect you against sexually transmitted diseases. She will also ask you if you use any method of birth control. If you were not using birth control at the time of the assault, she may offer you a morning-after pill to prevent pregnancy. If the hospital does not use morning-after pills, the doctor can tell you where you can get one.

The doctor or nurse will give you a pregnancy test and tests for sexually transmitted diseases. She will also tell you to have the tests taken again in two weeks. This is very important. Sexually transmitted diseases may not appear until two weeks after an assault.

Male victims of sexual assault also need medical attention. For a man, the hospital procedure will be the same, except for the pelvic exam. It is just as important for men to be checked and treated for sexually transmitted diseases and to have a follow-up exam two weeks later.

Some hospitals automatically contact the police in all cases of sexual assault. This does not mean that you have to make a police report. Only you can decide whether or not to report the assault to the police. If you do not want to report at that time, you can change your mind and go to the police later. Your medical records will be used as evidence.

Filing a Police Report and Pressing Charges

Your rape crisis counselor can also help you decide about going to the police. Rape is against the law. You may decide you want to report your rape to the police. You may decide you want to take your case to court. It's your decision. If you decide to go to the police, your rape crisis counselor will be able to tell you what to expect.

Telling your story to strangers and being questioned by police officers may be difficult, but ultimately it may make you feel more in control of circumstances and strong in your response. The police will take a report of what happened and open an investigation.

You may also want legal help. Again, your rape crisis counselor can tell you where to go. You will need to find a lawyer. You will need to tell your story in front of many people. Sometimes making people understand that forced sexual contact with someone you were on a date with or were regularly dating could qualify as rape is difficult. People often understand the criminal nature of rape when it's committed by a stranger more readily than when it's committed by an acquaintance or romantic partner. Attitudes are beginning to change about that as people become more enlightened concerning forced sexual relations among acquaintances, but stating your case to a jury and having them understand and believe you may still feel like a major hurdle to overcome. As difficult as this process may be, it can also be enormously empowering and can help restore your sense of strength, confidence, and security.

The sooner a sexual assault is reported, the more likely the rapist will be arrested and prosecution will be successful.

Recovering from date rape isn't easy, and it will take a long time. But recovery is possible. Most rape victims recover from their experiences and go on to live happy and successful lives. With the right support and counseling, healing will happen for you, too. It just takes patience, time, and hope.

five

WHAT CAN YOU DO IF A FRIEND IS RAPED?

If someone you love comes to you and says she has been raped, you may not know how to respond. Chances are you have never dealt with rape before and do not know what to say or do to comfort your friend. Be there for her and listen to what she has to say. Just be a friend. Here are some more guidelines:

Empathize

Listen closely to what your friend tells you. She needs understanding and support at this difficult time. Although you may not know what to say to help her, what she may need most at this time is just someone to listen to her and understand, support, and comfort her. You may help less by what you say than by what you let her say.

The victim of a date rape needs support and understanding more than anything else. Believe what she says, and convince her that you know it's not her fault.

Listen

Date rape victims are deep in the midst of a lot of confusing and often contradictory feelings. Talking about those feelings will help a victim cope with them. She may need to talk about it for a long time. She may need to talk about it more as time goes by. You don't need to say much. She just needs to know you're there and not growing impatient with her progress or weary of her needs.

Know How to Get Help

If your friend tells you she's been raped, find out what she's done about it. If she hasn't called a rape crisis center, encourage her to. If she's been injured, suggest she go to the hospital. If she wants to go to the police, help her get advice at a rape crisis center first. Date rape is very upsetting. Your friend will probably need some help in getting help. You can provide that assistance.

Support Her Decisions

If your friend doesn't want to go to the police, don't make her. If she does want to go to the police, help her do that. Date rape makes you doubt your judgment. Friends should support a victim's decisions. This will make the victim feel more in control. It will make her feel more confident. Don't try to force your friend to do anything. That will only make her think she really can't make decisions for herself. And remember, she has just been forced

Ten Great Questions to Ask About Date Rape

1 I was recently sexually assaulted. What should I do?

2 I am feeling a lot of different emotions after my experience. Is that normal?

3 A friend of mine has been assaulted. What can I do to help him/her?

4 Can a woman rape a man?

5 I know that being raped is never the victim's fault, but what can I do to make sure it doesn't happen again?

6 Can I receive medical and psychological services without my parents finding out?

7 Can I get pregnant from being raped? Can you do a pregnancy test yet? What are my options if I am pregnant?

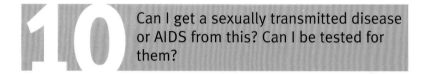

8 Is everything I tell you confidential?

9 Do I have to report this to the police immediately? What if I decide I want to report it months from now?

10 Can I get a sexually transmitted disease or AIDS from this? Can I be tested for them?

into sex after having her will ignored. Be sensitive to this fact and respect her desires at this very sensitive time.

It takes some date rape victims a long time to realize that they were raped. The rape may even have happened years ago. But when the victim realizes, acknowledges, and accepts what happened to her, she will need help. She will need just as much support as someone who was raped more recently. Be the same good and supportive friend to this kind of victim, too.

It's not easy to help a friend through a crisis. Especially when the crisis is something as awful as date rape. So be sure that you have support, too. Let someone know what you're going through. Otherwise, you might get upset and over-whelmed. Then you can't be a good friend. And if you feel that you're in over your head, get some advice from a rape coun-selor. She or he will tell you what to do next. You don't have to do this alone. Take care of yourself so you can take care of your friend.

A therapist can help you get on the path to recovery after a traumatic experience such as date rape.

Knowing the Facts

Date rape is a serious crime. It leaves victims hurt and confused, filled with a feeling of rage and betrayal that takes a long time to go away. Some survivors spend years trying to recover from the traumatic experience.

A lot of people mistakenly blame the victim of date rape. Some think she must have done something wrong or maybe she led the guy on. When someone is violated, and no one believes her, it only makes her feel worse. Very few reports of rape are false. It is something that not many people will lie about. Rape is never the victim's fault. It is a crime, and the criminal is at fault.

Knowing the facts about date rape will help you understand how and why rape happens. It will also help you to see the truth behind the many myths that surround rape. Rape does not discriminate. Anyone can be a victim of rape. Survivors need support and understanding from everyone.

acquaintance rape Forcing someone you know to have sex.

aggressive Pushy; being forceful to get what you want.

date rape Acquaintance rape that happens between two people who are dating.

feminine Having qualities that are regarded as characteristic of women or girls.

macho Like a he-man; tough.

media Newspapers, magazines, television, movies, radio, etc.

myth A belief not based on fact.

passive The opposite of aggressive; giving in to others.

rape Sex against someone's will.

rape counselor A person trained to help rape victims

rape crisis center A place where rape victims can get help.

sex object Something that exists only for sexual pleasure.

stereotypes Common beliefs about what all members of a group are like. These beliefs may or may not be true in individual cases.

An Abuse, Rape, and Domestic Violence Aid and Resource Collection
e-mail: aardvarcinfo@aol.com
Web site: http://www.aardvarc.org
 This nonprofit organization begun by survivors provides victims of rape, violence, and abuse information on how to end a violent relationship.

National Alliance to End Sexual Violence
1101 Vermont Avenue NW, Suite 400
Washington, DC 20005
Web site: http://www.naesv.org/index.html
 This national organization works on public policy and advocacy for victims of sexual assault.

National Center for Victims of Crime
2000 M Street NW, Suite 480
Washington, DC 20036
(800) FYI-CALL (394-2255)
Web site: http://www.ncvc.org/ncvc/Main.aspx
 This national organization deals with advocacy, education, and helping victims of crimes.

Planned Parenthood Federation of America
810 Seventh Avenue
New York, NY 10019

(800) 230-7526

Web site: http://www.ppfa.org/ppga/

Planned Parenthood–affiliated health centers nationwide provide high-quality, affordable reproductive health care and sexual health information to nearly five million women, men, and teens.

The Rape, Abuse, and Incest National Network (RAINN)
2000 L Street NW, Suite 406
Washington, DC 20036
(800) 656-HOPE (656-4673)
Web site: http://www.rainn.org

This is the nation's largest anti–sexual assault organization. It operates a hotline and does advocacy work.

Web Sites

Due to the changing nature of Internet links, Rosen Publishing has developed an online list of Web sites related to the subject of this book. This site is updated regularly. Please use this link to access the list:

http://www.rosenlinks.com/faq/dara

For Further Reading

Adams, Colleen. *Rohypnol: Roofies—"The Date Rape Drug."* New York, NY: Rosen Publishing, 2007.

Gedatus, Gustav Mark. *Date and Acquaintance Rape.* Mankato, MN: Lifematters, 2000.

Haley, James, ed. *Date Rape.* Farmington Hills, MI: Greenhaven Press, 2003.

Kehner, George B. *Date Rape Drugs.* New York, NY: Chelsea House Publications, 2004.

Landau, Elaine. *Date Violence.* New York, NY: Franklin Watts, 2005.

Lindquist, Scott. *The Date Rape Prevention Book: The Essential Guide for Girls and Women.* Naperville, IL: Sourcebooks, 2000.

Miklowitz, Gloria D. *Past Forgiving.* New York, NY: Simon & Schuster Children's Publishing, 1995.

Tatersall, Clare. *Date Rape Drugs.* New York, NY: Rosen Publishing, 2000.

Weyland, Jack. *Brittany.* Salt Lake City, UT: Deseret Book Company, 1997.

Williams, Mary E., ed. *Date Rape.* Farmington Hills, MI: Greenhaven Press, 1998.

Winkler, Kathleen. *Date Rape: A Hot Issue.* Berkeley Heights, NJ: Enslow Publishers, 1999.

Bibliography

Campus Violence Prevention Project. "Male Victims." University of Wisconsin. February 2006. Retrieved May 2006 (http://www.uwstout.edu/cvpp/male_page.html).

National Center for Injury Prevention and Control. "Intimate Partner Violence: Fact Sheet." CDC.gov. 2006. Retrieved May 2006 (http://www.cdc.gov/ncipc/factsheets/ipvfacts.htm).

National Center for Injury Prevention and Control. "Sexual Violence: Fact Sheet." CDC.gov. 2006. Retrieved May 2006 (http://www.cdc.gov/ncipc/factsheets/svfacts.htm).

National Center for Victims of Crime. "Male Rape." New York City Alliance Against Sexual Assault. 1997. Retrieved May 2006 (http://www.nycagainstrape.org/survivors_factsheet_38.html).

Rape, Abuse, and Incest National Network. "Statistics." RAINN.org. 2006 Retrieved May 2006. (http://www.rainn.org/statistics/index.html).

"Sexual Abuse Statistics." Prevent-Abuse-Now.com. 2006. Retrieved May 2006 (http://www.prevent-abuse-now.com/stats.htm).

Index

Photo Credits

Cover © www.istockphoto.com/Jim Pruitt; p. 5 © Mika/zefa/Corbis;
p. 6 © www.istockphoto.com/Jamie Wilson; p. 9 © Chris Jackson/Getty
Images; p. 11 © Mario Tama/Getty Images; p. 13 © Jimin Lai/AFP/
Getty Images; p. 19 © Fred Prouser/Reuters/Corbis; p. 22 © David
Friedman/Getty Images; p. 24 by Antonio Mari; p. 26 © Graeme
Robertson/Getty Images; p. 29 © www.istockphoto.com/Nick Roberts;
p. 33 © Bob Mahoney/Time Life Pictures/Getty Images; p. 34 ©
Amanda Edwards/Getty Images; p. 38 © www.istockphoto.com/Rasmus
Rasmussen; p. 40 © www.istockphoto.com/Cristal Goodman; p. 43 ©
www.istockphoto.com/Alain Juteau: p. 45 © www.istockphoto.com/
Marcin Balcerzak; p. 49 © www.istockphoto.com/Frances Twitty; p. 52
© www.istockphoto.com/Oleg Prikhodko; p. 56 © VOISIN/PHANIE/
Photo Researchers, Inc.

Designer: Evelyn Horovicz